Change the World

Written by Tuleen Ziben

Illustrated by MediaLab

To Her.

Change the world I thought.
Change the world,
Why not?

The world's too big to change
they said,
Not as big as the world
I see in my head.

Change the world?
They mocked,
A girl like you cannot.

Wait and see, I said.
I'll make the world better
I bet!

Change the world?
They mocked,
A girl like you cannot.

Prove them wrong I will.
I'll make the world better still.

Change the world?
They mocked,
A girl like you cannot.

As their voices grew louder,
Mine lost its power.

Change the world?
I mocked,
A girl like me cannot.

The world's too big to change,
I said...

Then I remembered...

It's not as big as the world
I see in my head.

Change the world I thought,
Change the world?
People will mock,

But their voices will
be quiet now in my head,
From now on I'll listen to
only my voice instead.

Change the world I thought,
Change the world I am,
Every moment of every day,
I'll make the world better my way.

The End.

Written by Tuleen Ziben
Illustrated by MediaLab

Made in United States
Cleveland, OH
09 March 2025

15021699R00019